The Thrill of Victory
and
The Agony of
Defeat

RANDY CLARK

Apostolic Network of Global Awakening
1451 Clark Street
Mechanicsburg, PA 17055

Unless otherwise noted, Scripture quotations are taken from HOLY BIBLE,
NEW INTERNATIONAL VERSION®. Copyright © 1973, 1978, 1984 by International Bible Society. Used by permission of Zondervan Publishing House.

Third Printing: January 2014

ISBN 978-0-9844966-7-9

For more information on how to order this book or any of the other materi-
als that Global Awakening offers, please contact:

Apostolic Network of Global Awakening
1451 Clark Street
Mechanicsburg, PA 17055
1-866-AWAKENING
www.globalawakeningstore.com

Table of Contents

{ The Agony of Defeat }

Why doesn't everyone experience healing when we pray for them? How do we keep going when those we pray for don't get well? What is the cost of healing ministry, and how can we bear it?

Cost of Healing

Healing ministry is costly. Make no mistake about it. When you receive impartation for healing, you commit yourself to embrace suffering. Healing is part of the cross Jesus calls us to take up when we follow Him.

After pointing out that he would be rejected, killed and then raised to life, in Luke 9:23, Jesus said, "...If anyone would come after me, he must deny himself and take up his cross daily and follow me."

In our culture, the cross has lost a lot of its power as an image because we have seen it so often in jewelry or adorning steeples. But in Jesus' day, the cross was understood as a horrible object of suffering.

Jesus' disciples knew to take up a cross meant to experience personal suffering. Healing is in that cross.

Commanded to Heal

Why do I believe that? Jesus commanded his church to heal. The church is the body of Christ. The church is to be what He was. We are to continue his ministry in the great commission given in Matthew 28:19-20: "Therefore go and make disciples of all nations, baptizing them in the name of the Father and of the Son and of the Holy Spirit and teaching them to obey everything I have commanded you..."

Earlier in his ministry, when Jesus commissioned his 12 disciples and when he sent forth 72 others, He commanded them to preach the good news of the Kingdom, to heal the sick and to cast out demons. In Matthew 10, He even said to raise the dead. All those things are happening today.

However, one of the problems in the church of Jesus Christ today is that we are very much like the first century Jewish religious leaders. Jesus came to them and said, "You have let go of the commands of God and are holding on to the traditions of men." (Mark 7:8).

We are commanded to heal the sick and to cast out demons. Yet large portions of the church don't realize we have been commanded to do this. They don't even believe we are supposed to do it. They believe that's all over and not for us today. So because of the traditions of men, the word of God has been set aside.

God's Truth or Our Experience?

Once I was in Florence, Kentucky, at the second largest Assembly of God Church in the state. I was reading from Matthew 10:2 and didn't like that part about raising the dead because it embarrassed me. In fact, I would lower my voice when I got to that part, but the Lord called me on it.

The Lord said, "You are embarrassed by that aren't you?" I said, "Yes I am. I'm embarrassed by that. God, I am still struggling with seeing the sick get healed let alone the dead get raised."

I then heard one of the strongest rebukes I've ever heard from the Holy Spirit to me personally. This is what He said, and I can still quote it to this day: "Don't you dare lower my word to the level of your experience. Don't you be an experienced-based preacher. Do not create a theology that excuses your lack. Do not create a theology based on your experience of not seeing the dead raised or people healed. Preach my word and let people's experience rise to it." Whoa!

So I taught for the first time publicly about how to raise the dead, based not upon my experience, but through the stories I knew from other people who had done it. In that meeting, a man heard those words, remembered them and used that prayer to bring his boy back to life when he was killed in an accident a few months later.

Persisting Through Defeat

This booklet contains not the stories of victory, but the stories of defeat. Do I want to discourage you? No, absolutely not. I want to encourage you to keep praying regardless of how many defeats you experience.

When I go around the country, I meet a lot of people who used to pray for the sick who no longer do. Why not? People say they believe God heals today, but they've stopped praying for healing. Why? Because they've experienced failure. I don't like doing something I fail at a lot. Probably you don't either. But the truth of the matter is this: if you have a healing ministry, you have a lot of failure.

This isn't the message I share at meetings when I am trying to get the sick healed. It doesn't build faith for healing. But it is the truth that I want those who are going to pray for others to be healed to understand.

If you are going to pray to see people healed, you are also going to see people who don't get healed. You will weep over their heartbreaking, emotional stories. Here is the painful truth: I honestly believe I have prayed for more people who have not been healed than anyone reading this booklet.

It's important for you to understand that there is suffering involved with this ministry. Very simply, the reason why more Christians don't pray for the sick is that we don't like to feel pain. We want someone to tell us what we can do to have a better life with as little pain as possible.

Defeats and Victories Go Hand in Hand

When Jesus invites you into the healing ministry, it's an invitation to experience defeat as well as victory. Years ago, the ABC network broadcast the *ABC Wide World of Sports* on Sunday nights. Every week it opened with the words "The thrill of victory and the agony of defeat." The video would show someone winning a race and then a guy on a big ski jump crashing or some other painful defeat. That is the most perfect illustration of the healing ministry I can think of.

After 20 years in this ministry, I promise you that if you will pray for the sick, you will have thrills of victory, but I also promise that you will experience agonies of defeat. I have a lot of stories to share—most of which occurred over a six-month period—and they are all painful. But here's the point. Don't let your defeats stop you from praying or you won't have any victories.

4

Some time ago, I met a man whose adult daughter died. He hadn't prayed for a person since his daughter died. He somehow blamed himself that she hadn't been healed. He came and listened to one of the messages I gave. Afterwards, he said I gave him back the right to start praying for the sick again. And from that day on he began to do so.

Embracing Suffering

To pray for the sick, to see them healed, you must be willing to embrace suffering. You must be willing to say, "I will embrace the cross of Luke 9:23." You must say, "I will knowingly embrace a ministry that will bring suffering into my life."

For most of us in our Christian walk in America, there is no suffering. But if you pray for the sick, there is a high emotional price tag that you will have to pay. Praying for healing touches your heart. You need power to persevere. Sometimes you will feel you can't go on because it's too much to bear. This is one of the most difficult ministries you could ever have. You must be prepared to handle failure. You must be willing to say "I don't know" when people don't get healed.

Why did this person get healed and that one didn't? "I don't know." Why did that sinner get healed and that pillar in the church die of the same thing? "I don't know."

To be involved in healing ministry you must be willing to embrace emotional suffering and be willing to say "I don't know." These are the two critical requirements.

Here's the heart of the matter. If you don't pray for the sick, whom is the Lord going to use? Those who have been taught cessation and that sign gifts are not for today? Those who believe that nothing supernatural ever did happen, including the parting of the Red Sea, which means that the Egyptians drowned in six inches of water in a reed sea?

The problem is, even amongst those churches that do believe in healing ministry, very few are involved in it. The reason why is: it hurts. It costs too much. Healing ministry will bring you some of the most joyous experiences of your life, but you will have more times that you will go home and cry.

Power and Compassion

If we want to be involved in healing ministry, we must pray for two things: more power and more compassion. If we get power but don't have compassion, our ministry will not reflect Jesus. We need both God's heart and God's power to go along with it.

So I am praying to God for three things: "I ask you to keep me humble, give me your compassion and your heart for the lost and the sick and give me the power of your anointing to do something about it."

The guy that came to my Baptist church to lead our first healing workshop said this: "Don't say this doesn't work until you have prayed for at least 200 people because some of you will start praying for the sick and will not see anybody healed a few times and will quit. But I am telling you, do not quit or say you did not get anything until you have laid your hands on 200 people and you, yourself have prayed for them. If you will do that, I promise you will be hooked for life because you will see people get healed."

Perseverance in Prayer

How many people would you be willing to pray for that don't get healed to see a woman only 49 years old who is losing her mind to Parkinson's be totally healed and given back to her husband? How many people would you be willing to pray for that don't get healed to see a little boy whose nerves were gone, destroyed and deaf be totally restored? How many people would you be willing to pray for that don't get healed to see a mother who is in her 20's dying of an inoperable brain tumor be healed by God?

Are you willing to embrace the pain and suffering in order to experience the thrill of victory? I don't know how to explain it except I know that when I read that Semple "Sister Amy" McPherson would see thousands get healed, yet weep for the majority of the stretchers that came on ambulances and left on ambulances. One of the agonies of a healing ministry is what you didn't see happen.

If the people you are praying for are members of your church, it's even harder. The more you know them and the more you love them, the more pain you feel if they don't get healed.

In the church, when a pastor dies or a staff leader, an elder, or somebody that everybody knows and respects and you have fought, fasted and done everything you knew for them and they still didn't get healed, there is great pain. Two things can happen. First, the church can back away from praying for healing. They still have the doctrine on the books but not in their hearts anymore. Or second, the church becomes angry—not at God but at the devil. The believers become more determined to come into a greater place of anointing so as not to lose more of their young men and young women to leukemia, cancer or whatever took the one they loved.

Before I became an evangelist, I pastored for 32 years. I know what it is like as a pastor to see some of your key leaders die. Here is some bad news for you. The devil does not abide by the Geneva Convention. You say, "I don't want to get involved in this because I don't want the attack." I tell you the devil doesn't care whether you are fighting or not fighting him. He comes to kill, steal and destroy. So, we had better learn how to fight.

Responding to God's Call

In Exodus 3:7-8, God said to Moses, "...I have indeed seen the misery of my people in Egypt. I have heard them crying out because of their slave drivers, and I am concerned about their suffering. So I have come down to rescue them from the hand of the Egyptians..." And in verse 10, "So now, go. I am sending you to Pharaoh to bring my people the Israelites out of Egypt." I am praying as you read the stories in this booklet that the Holy Spirit will touch you and cause you to see and hear the cry of his people who are in bondage because of illnesses and infirmities.

If Jesus Christ is the same yesterday, today and forever more and if He loved to heal the sick and cast out demons, doesn't He still want to through his body today? The answer is "Yes." Who can God use if not us? We must respond to his call. We can't be sidelined by the emotional pain. We must be strengthened by the Holy Spirit. We must be willing to come to the cross of the healing ministry of Jesus Christ. We must say "Yes" despite the pain.

Boy Without A Brain

In 1994, soon after I'd received a prophecy on being used in the healing ministry, I went to New Jersey. We held meetings at a church with 700 in attendance. It was powerful. But on Sunday morning, I felt like the Lord said, "Don't preach here."

Instead he sent us to preach at a little church where there were only 20 people. After the service, a young woman in her 20's came forward with her little boy, about two years old. He had been born with no brain, just the stem, and he couldn't communicate. He'd never even been able to acknowledge that she was his mother. She told me her husband left her after her son was born. She came because she heard I would be there, and she was hoping God would give her a miracle. I prayed for over an hour for this child while his mother told me how hard it had been for her and the burden she had with the father gone. I prayed and prayed. But the little boy didn't get healed.

Boy with Muscular Disorder

Later that same Sunday, one of the pastors at the larger church came to me and said, "Randy, we just want you to know there have been so many healings, and the faith has gone so high that parents are going to the institutions and getting their children out of the institutions that they do not take into public because the birth defects are so severe, and they are bringing them to the meeting tonight." Did I think, "Oh boy, that's good."? No! I thought, "Oh, my gosh."

The place was packed when I walked into the meeting. Right in front of me was a little boy, 9 to 11 years old, and he had a rare disease that had destroyed all the muscle tissue — a terminal disease. He looked like a skeleton wrapped in skin, he was so skinny. The music played, and he was shaking this one leg to the beat of the music. I was overwhelmed with the compassion of God. While we worshipped for 45 minutes, I stood behind him and prayed for him. Often I will do that in meetings when I see somebody very, very ill or terminal who cannot wait that long. I pray for them while worship is going on.

After I prayed for him 45 minutes, he wasn't healed. I always thought nothing had happened until I learned about eight years later that he was still alive, and no one with his disease had ever lived that long. In a sense, the disease stopped right at that point. He wasn't healed, but something did happen.

Teen with Spina Bifida

The meeting continued, and I gave the message on healing. Then the doors opened up in the back, and a mother and father in their early 30's came in with their teenage son strapped to a gurney. They pushed the gurney up to the front while I watched. As they pushed the gurney, it was clear that the mother and father, who had gone to the institution to get this boy and bring him, hoped that the man of God would be used of God to bring a healing to their son, and I felt the weight of that.

The boy thrashed on the gurney and made loud verbal noises. During the interview I found out that he had spina bifida. The shunt the doctors put in collapsed and kinked, causing massive brain damage. He went from being communicative with spina bifida to a spastic no longer able to communicate. Mom and Dad looked at me with hope that God would use me to raise up and restore their son. I felt their hope. I felt their expectation. I felt the weight of their desire for God to use me. I prayed and prayed, and after a while as nothing happened, the weight of all the hopes and expectations increased. The boy didn't get healed.

That was 1994, and I can't forget it. I can't remember any of the ones that were healed that night, and there were hundreds healed. But I can't forget that teenager on the gurney, the boy who was skin and bones and the little boy without a brain.

Boy in a Wheelchair

I left New Jersey and went to Knoxville, Tennessee. A few days later the Lord spoke to me and said, "You are not going to see people in wheelchairs be healed unless you pray for them more." There were about a thousand people in the meeting in Knoxville, and scores if not hundreds were healed.

About midnight, I saw a 14-year-old boy in a wheelchair. Now I have a problem with a very weak stomach. But I thank God that He gave me a very poor sense of smell because smells can make me sick real easy. When I drew close to the 14-year-old boy, I could smell the strong smell of urine. I thought, "What would Jesus do?" He wouldn't be repulsed. He would push through because of his love. So I knelt down beside the boy and asked his name and what was wrong with him. He had spina bifida and no control of his bladder. He needed a miracle. We prayed for his miracle.

At midnight his diaper was full and it smelled badly, but I knew that Jesus would not stop because of that and so I continued praying and praying for him. After 15 or 20 minutes, he looked at me and said, "You know I am from a family that my mom and dad adopted children and every one of us have birth defects. My sister is over there. Tonight may not be my night. I will go with you, and let's go pray for my sister."

Girl with Cerebral Palsy

So I walked, and he rolled his wheelchair to his sister who was born with cerebral palsy. I prayed for his sister with cerebral palsy. After I prayed for a while, the girl said, "I want to try to walk." I have seen this so many times. I helped her up, and we started to walk. She would take a step and one toe would catch behind the other foot. I would reach down and pull it out while all the time praying for her. She took another step, and the same thing happened all the way across the stage and back. She then collapsed into her wheelchair, and she wasn't healed.

Blind Girl

Next, I went to High Point, North Carolina to preach at a healing conference. During the invitation, lots of people came up and were healed, but what I remember are these three 12- year-old girls, two brunettes and one blonde. My daughter was about that age at the time. If you're a father and have a daughter, your heart can be so captured by your daughter. I was thinking they are so full of faith.

I thought maybe the blonde girl had a toothache. I asked her what she wanted prayer for. She looked up at me and said, "I am blind." Nothing looked wrong with her eyes. I said, "You are blind! How?" She said, "When I was six years old in kindergarten, I had this rare disease and lost my sight. I believe Jesus can heal me."

I prayed for her three sessions each day. I prayed for her more than I prayed for anyone else. I prayed longer for her every session. She came so expectant. I would say, "Is anything happening?" She would say, "I think I am beginning to see." I would say, "Can you see my fingers?" She would say, "Not yet, but I think I am beginning to see."

This happened for three days until the last session, when I said, "Can you see my fingers?" She said, "No." At that moment, she realized she wasn't being healed, and I made a mistake, and so will you. We are just humans, and we make mistakes and errors in judgment.

My heart was so drawn to this 12-year-old girl. I didn't use wisdom and said something to her that actually made it worse. I reached down and took her in my arms and whispered in her ear. Grace was her name. I said, "Grace, I so wanted you to be able to see what a beautiful young woman you are becoming." She spun around and threw her arms around her mother's waist, shaking and weeping as her mom cried, too, and I walked away with tears running down my cheeks.

That was in 1995, and I can't forget her name. A friend saw me, and said, "She got behind your shield." I said, "Yes, she did." Like a doctor or nurse, when you do this type of work, it is almost like you have a shield to guard your heart against pain. You want to love, but you have to get up and do it tomorrow, and you don't want to be burned out because you get so emotionally involved with those you pray for.

People have condemned me, saying I shouldn't have a shield. Wait until you have prayed for about 10,000 or 20,000 people. Then come and tell me that. Several years ago, Grace sent me a Christmas card with a note that said, "I'm still believing for my healing, and don't you be discouraged. You keep praying for the sick."

Woman with Head Injury

I traveled to a large church in Anderson, Indiana. As I was preaching and the crowd was standing there during the invitation, I was drawn to a very tall handsome young man. I have learned to pay attention to these things. I don't understand why, but I knew something was wrong.

After the invitation, and we start praying for the sick, I walked straight to him. When I reached him, I understood. Beside him in a wheelchair sat the remains of a beautiful young bride in her 20's. She had a big hole in the side of her head where the skull had not even been put back and it was concaved in and the saliva was dripping down her chin. Her husband who said for better or worse, for richer or poorer, in sickness and in health had a washcloth that he used to wipe the saliva going down her chin. He was there because he desperately hoped that I would be the one God would use to restore his bride to him. I prayed and prayed, but she was not healed.

Girl with Parkinson's Disease

Next I visited a church in northwest Indiana that believed in healing. There I told the story of a 49-year-old woman who was totally restored from Parkinson's disease. The next night a 12-year-old girl came forward. Actually her dad brought her and had to stand behind her to hold her up because she could no longer stand on her own. She wanted me to pray for her because she had heard the testimony about the healing from Parkinson's. This girl at 12 was the youngest person in the United States with Parkinson's. I concentrated on praying for her; my team prayed for almost everyone else. I prayed for that girl every session, 30 minutes to one hour each time, but she didn't get healed.

When I was praying for her, I could see her hope dwindling, and she moved into despair and began crying and her nose started running. Somebody gave her a handkerchief, and she was struggling to try to wipe her own nose. Her Mom and

Dad were standing there, remembering the testimony I told about the woman healed from Parkinson's, and the girl was remembering also, but there was no healing for her. How do you handle that?

Power for Miracles

Ten years before, when I first started praying for the sick, I went on a 40-day fast asking God to give me an anointing for healing, and I received an increase. I am not a person that fasts. Matter of fact, after I finished that one 40-day fast, I never fasted another day until ten years later.

But from the experience of these failures, I began to say, "Oh God, the anointing that I have right now is not enough. It's not enough to have an anointing for healing. All these conditions need miracles. Something has been destroyed that must be created or something is there that must be destroyed. It isn't healing these people need. They need miracles. I need the power for miracles."

Then I began the second 40-day fast of my life. I wasn't being religious. I was desperate because my heart was being ripped out. I was praying, "God, I want to see miracles." By the way, it was on the 23rd day of that fast that the 49-year-old woman was healed of Parkinson's, the first miracle.

That year I went on many extended fasts, and then I didn't fast again for quite some time. But why did I need more anointing? Did I want more anointing so I could just have a good time and laugh and be drunk? No, I wanted people to receive the miracles they so desperately needed and I longed for them to have, whatever the cost.

I liked what Bill Johnson said after the anointing power fell on him, and he looked like a spastic lying in bed with no control of his arms and legs. He said he felt like God said, "Would you be willing to bear the stigma of being a spastic for the anointing?" Bill said he thought about having no control of his legs or arms and could see himself going down the streets of Redding that way and trying to explain that God did that to him. God said, "Would you be willing to bear the stigma?" And lying there with tears running down his face, Bill said, "If this is what it costs to have more Lord, I would be willing to bear this." He meant it.

So the question remains. Are we willing to pay the cost to receive the anointing, to receive more, to serve God and bring healing and miracles to his people?

Pressing In and Persevering

There are not a whole lot of people lining up in the Kingdom to carry this cross. I will tell you that. We have created theological excuses and rationalizations. I think it's even possible that we experience the influence of demons who want to rob the church of its power.

But I tell you this: I never saw any stroke victims healed until after twenty years of praying for stroke victims. I never saw any stroke victims healed until I heard about the dead being raised in Mozambique, and that testimony gave me a greater degree of faith. Then in 24 hours we saw three stroke victims healed.

I never saw an AIDS victim healed until just recently, and then we saw three in one year. I never saw a paraplegic healed until just two years ago. I saw my first deaf person healed about six years ago, and now in one month we saw

80 deaf healed. It was more than 25 years before we saw the first blind person healed, but in one month last year we saw 20 blind healed. I only prayed for a couple of them. Our ministry team prayed for the rest.

Going Deeper

I know God wants us to go deeper. I am not saying these miracles are the greatest thing God has ever done. As a matter of fact, I am saying we haven't even yet attained the miracles experienced in the 1948 healing revival. But I believe that the Bible teaches that in the last days we will experience the greatest revival ever seen. It will not be The Laodicean Church of Revelation 3. It will not be the lukewarm church, but it will be the church on fire.

It will be a time of great darkness and great light. It will be a time of great persecution that will cause the great falling away. But it will also be a time of great harvest because every time that there is martyrdom, there is release of fire and power and evangelism. In the last days, we are not going to be a weak church. We are going to be a strong church.

I do believe that the glory in the latter house shall be greater than the former. I honestly believe with all my heart that there is another great healing revival that God wants to bring and another great missionary wave that he wants to send out. These missionaries will go with a strong commitment to healing and deliverance.

I believe we are moving into that time right now, and God wants to anoint his church. But it is not an anointing of superficiality, and it is not a call for impartation so that you can have fun. This call is to embrace the cross of Jesus, to love as He loved, to feel as He felt and to ask Him to anoint you with power. It is to ask for a Baptism of the Holy Spirit, as Gordon Fee says, to give you the power to work miracles and the power to walk through the darkness when the miracle doesn't come.

{ The Thrill of Victory }

I once asked somebody, "What's the healing ministry like?" The answer is simple: It's thrilling and it's agonizing.

That old ABC Wide World of Sports intro perfectly describes the healing ministry—the thrill of victory as someone wins and the agony of defeat as a guy crashes from a huge ski jump. Do you remember that? What a picture of healing ministry because there are thrills of victories, and there are agonies of defeat.

Pastors have told me that the message I share on the agonies of defeat is one of the most helpful messages they have ever been taught. But when I am trying to build faith for healing, I focus on the thrill of victory, never denying the defeats, but emphasizing the victories.

The whole point of this two-part booklet is for you to believe that God can use you. That you personally can experience the thrill of victory.

Five Principles for Healing

I am going to give you five principles. Each of these is true, but if you turn these principles into laws, they will backfire.

Actually, the devil takes the law and beats you up with it, if you turn a biblical principle into a law. Then when you feel like you are falling short of the law, you feel unqualified or disqualified for God to use you. So, your expectation is actually lower. The enemy uses this legal concept to lower your expectations. You feel that you are not meeting the conditions and therefore you don't qualify for greater results.

Before we get into those principles, I want you to say these words out loud: God can use little ole me. Repeat it: God can use little ole me. Say it again: God can use little ole me. One more time: God can use little ole me! If you believe that simple truth more when you've finished reading this booklet than you do now, then I will have succeeded in my purpose in writing it.

Are you ready? I am going to give you five principles that are true, but they are not laws. So, every one of the illustrations I use for each principle will contradict it to prove it is not an iron-clad law. I want you to remember that even when you feel like you are not meeting the conditions, your faith is not limited. I want you to understand that God can still move even when one of the principles isn't there.

The principles are true, but the important thing is that God is bigger than the principles. Ultimately, He is the sovereign Lord of the Universe, and you never know what He is going to do sometimes. I know this can be confusing, but the important point to understand, that you need to get within you, is that mercy triumphs over judgment.

First, I will give you the principles and then share the stories. Some people like principles and points set out directly. This is for you. If you understand them, you can be satisfied and walk away.

For those who can't remember the points, you will have the stories, and you will not forget what the points represent because you will remember them through the stories.

The Principle of Faith

The first and most important principle is the principle of faith. In Matthew 9:22, Jesus told the woman with the issue of blood, "Take heart, daughter, your faith has healed you."

In Matthew 9:29, Jesus told two blind men, "According to your faith will it be done to you," and their sight was restored. It is all about faith. If you have faith, you can speak to the mountain, and it will be thrown into the sea. If you have faith, you can speak to the mulberry tree, and it will be uprooted, if you have faith and do not doubt. Jesus spoke to a tree, and it withered overnight.

The very famous passage in Mark 11:21-24 deals with this tree and the importance of faith. Peter calls attention to the withered tree, remembering that Jesus had cursed it. Jesus responds, "Have faith in God. I tell you the truth, if anyone says to this mountain, 'Go, throw yourself into the sea,' and does not doubt in his heart but believes that what he says will happen, it will be done for him. Therefore, I tell you, whatever you ask for in prayer, believe that you have received it, and it will be yours."

Sometimes we have difficulties with scripture. And it is not because the scripture is so obscure. This scripture is as plain as day. The real problem is coming to walk in the reality of this scripture. The challenge before the Church is not understanding something difficult, but walking in light of the truth of scriptures that are really clear and plain when they give us invitations and promises, but we often fall so short of walking in their reality. That is the real challenge for me.

Hebrews 11:6 says that "without faith it is impossible to please God." Further, I believe that based upon the best in medical science today, God, our Creator, created us in such a way that our bodies are hard-wired to respond to faith. Because God loves us so much, He has formed us so that our bodies can and do respond to faith. The placebo effect is proof of this.

So, the principle is this: Wherever there is more faith, more happens. Wherever there is great faith, great things happen. Wherever there are more people of faith, more things happen in that congregation than in a congregation where there is less faith.

Jesus himself could do no mighty deeds in Nazareth because of the unbelief of the people there. Faith is important. Now, I would rather be around people with more faith than I have than less faith than I have. I don't want to be hanging around people who are questioning God. I want to hang around people who are bragging on God. I don't want to surround myself with doubters and listen to their voices. I want to surround myself with people who have seen the dead raised and raised the dead. I want to be around people who have seen and done exploits for God. I want my faith to grow.

But having said that, I caution you to move out of grace. Beyond every principle in this booklet, the most important thing to understand is grace. The gift of healing is a charisma, from which we get the word "charismatic." "Charisma" is a Greek word. And it literally means a grace, an expression of grace. It is just the grace of God manifested, the Kingdom breaking through, mercy triumphing over judgment and grace being released.

Grace is an enablement, a divine empowerment to accomplish something. So all our ministry is grace-based.

John Wimber taught me this: When you stand praying for somebody, don't step off the rug of peace. What did he mean? Remember that this is grace. Remember that it is God who does it; you can't do it.

So, pray with confidence and speak to the condition. At the same time, remember that you don't have to rev yourself up. You don't have to try to work up your spirit, your soul, to get it to happen. If you try to pray by working yourself up, four things may happen: One, you get tired more quickly; two, you wear out; three, you lose your voice yelling; and four, often you will miss a word from the Lord in the midst of your emotionalism.

I am an emotional person. I think that emotions are good. God made emotions for us. There are toxic emotions and there are good emotions, and I am not against emotions. If I lived in the 1500's, they would call me an enthusiast because I believe that God speaks to us, and I want to experience it all. So, I am not against emotion, but I am against this belief that if we become emotional, God will move more than if we are quiet in our spirits and standing on the rug of peace knowing it is not my effort that matters, but that God is looking just for faith. That's not always easy because sometimes I want to see it so much that I can feel myself striving instead of resting.

Man with Neck Injury

Let me tell you a story. In Melbourne, Florida, I had a revival for eight months. There was a pastor there who had the same first name as me—Randy Ostrander. He had started a church in Melbourne, Florida, and it had grown in a few years to an average attendance of 600. He was an athlete and I believe, still held the high hurdles record. He had been a pro football draft choice. He was a hero locally for his athletic abilities.

However, one day when he was younger, he was working out, pushing weights, and the machine broke, and the weights fell down across his neck doing severe damage. He had had three vertebrae fused during different surgeries, and he was still in uncontrollable pain despite taking the highest pain medication possible. And he had been this way for six years. For six years he could not be around anything loud. He had the equivalent of a terrible migraine headache every waking moment of his life for six years. He was totally disabled. He couldn't play with his kids, and he had to resign the church.

Here's the thing: He was a Word of Faith pastor, and he had a faith school of healing in his church. He went to some of the most famous healing people in that movement to be prayed for—Kenneth Hagin and others. But he hadn't been healed.

He had been prayed for over 100 times and hadn't been healed. He had believed, and he stood in faith, and he came to the meeting, and I prayed for him, and absolutely nothing happened. The next day he set up a meeting with me and his wife, and he told me the whole story.

As I share this story, I want you to understand that lots of people come to me, and they don't get healed. That happens to other people who pray for healing, too. I don't mean anything negative about anybody that I just mentioned; it is just a reality. Everybody has people that they pray for who don't get healed.

Don't be discouraged—if you are the one praying or the one asking for healing. Just because someone prays for you and you don't get healed that time doesn't mean you are not going to get healed. But this may not be the time. I don't know why, and I don't have an answer for it, either.

Anyway, Randy Ostrander told me his dilemma. He was on high dosages of medication, but it was still not working. So he had started taking his medicine with whiskey to try to cut the pain. His doctors had switched his medication because they said he was going to become addicted to it. Yet he was in such severe pain.

So, he told me, he'd been prayed for so many times, but he felt he couldn't go on. And he asked me, "Should I just accept this and try to be the best Christian that I can with this disease?" At the time, I was a Vineyard pastor and he was a Word of Faith pastor, and he asked me that.

I said, "You know, Randy, I understand. And there are going to be times that you don't want to get prayed for because you are discouraged—people do get discouraged when they've had diseases for a long time. So you may not feel up to being prayed for at every service. Sometimes you just won't have any expectation for healing, but when you do, don't stop getting prayed for. When you have expectations, get prayer because you have nothing to lose and everything to gain even though you haven't been healed yet. So I encourage you to keep getting prayer."

Well, because of his headaches, he couldn't be in the meeting during worship, so he came after the second night, after the meeting was over, when we were praying for the sick. He came up to me and he told me, "I am supposed to go to Johns Hopkins to have another surgery on my neck, a fourth fusion in my neck. I already can't look up and see the stars. I can't look down and see my shoes. I can't look to the left or to the right. All I can do is move my eyes up and down, left and right, and even when I do that, you can hear the grinding in my neck." And I could hear it.

He came, and his boy was with him, and his wife was with him. He said, "You know, I am in so much pain I am not a good father anymore. I am not a good husband anymore. When you are constantly gritting your teeth because you are under the pain, your attitude, your mood can be so bad. I am embarrassed how miserable I am in some ways and sometimes how I treat my own family. I don't want to, it's just that I hurt so much." So, he told me, "You have got to pray for me! I can't have another surgery!"

Now, I wished that he hadn't told me that morning that he didn't have any faith left. I wished that he hadn't told me that he was ready to give up. I wished that he hadn't told me that he was in that state because I was thinking, "Oh, my gosh!"

I knew where he was at spiritually. Faith-wise he had almost given up. So his wife was there and she was praying. She told me later, "Do you know what I was praying for when you were praying, Randy?" I said, "What were you praying?" She said, "I was praying that you wouldn't be discouraged when he wasn't healed." And don't blame her. Wait until you have waited six years and seen your husband prayed for over 100 times by some of the most important people in the Christian world, and he is still hurting. And everything that you had taught and believed hasn't manifested yet.

So Randy Ostrander said, "There is my 16-year-old boy. He has not had a dad for six years. I have got to be healed." The "got to be healed" wasn't faith; it was desperation.

So I said, "Okay. I will pray." Now, how do you know if you have faith for healing? Do you know how you know? I'll tell you how. It is not what you believe; it is what you do. If you don't pray for healing, you don't have any faith for healing. All you have is doctrinal assent. But if you have real faith for healing, you will pray for people. Whether or not they get healed, you still have faith for healing because you are doing it.

Some people will argue all day, claiming that God can heal today, but they never pray for people to be healed. All they have is an argument; they don't have any faith. Sometimes you know whether or not you have a great faith in the moment or a little bit of faith. Inside my Bible, I have a mustard seed taped to remind me how little it is. And so I had my mustard seed, that much faith.

How did I know I had faith? Because I was going to pray. I hadn't quit praying for the sick. I am still praying for the sick, but there are times when you have great faith and times when your faith is not so big.

So Randy Ostrander had all of this severe pain. He had headaches. He had fused vertebrae in his neck. And I didn't even have the faith to start praying for his neck, and I knew I didn't. But then I remembered that morning I had been awakened by a mental picture of a radiating pain, a picture, really, of pain going down the left arm.

So, I said, "Randy, do you happen to have pain going down your left arm?" He said, "I do. From the pinched nerve in my neck I have pain, burning pain, going down this arm." I said, "I am going to pray for your arm, and I am going to pray for the pain." That is where I started because I thought that would be the easiest starting point. So, I began praying, and he said, "I am feeling God." My mustard seed got bigger. I kept praying, and he said, "My arm—the pain—it is getting better." My faith got bigger.

I prayed some more, and he said, "All the pain just left my arm." My faith got bigger. I started praying then for the migraine headaches. As I started praying for the migraine headaches, he said, "I have got power like electricity. I feel heat on my head." My faith got bigger. I was praying, and he said, "For the first time in six years, for the first time in six years, I have no headache!" My faith went WHAM!!! You would have thought that I had graduated from Rhema at this point.

I said, "I command that pain to leave the neck. I bless this neck in Jesus' name." And he jumped up. His wife was crying. He grabbed his son, and I was jumping and twirling around. I didn't know that is what the Bible says in Hebrews. One of the words for praise is to jump up and twirl. I didn't know that, but I am sure that they got that word from watching what people did when they got excited with God. They created that word—jump up and twirl—praise God—when they saw people jumping up and twirling.

So, I was jumping and twirling, and I came down and a woman grabbed me and said, "Now, pray for me." I thought, "Well I didn't even get to celebrate very long. Here is another one."

Woman with Parkinson's

Sometimes we don't want to pray for people. One time at another meeting, I was focused on impartation, primarily for young people, so I directed everybody who was over 29 and needed healing to go to the balcony where there was a ministry team so they could receive healing prayer. It was the only time in a series of meetings that I planned not to pray for the sick.

So, I was not expecting to pray for healing for anyone, but Ann Harrison came up to me. She looked like she was 60 years old or older, and she was really only 49. She was shaking, and I just thought that the anointing of God was on her because there was a whole lot of shaking going on there anyway.

She came up to me and said, "I want you to pray for me." I said, "No, you are over 29 years old, so you go on up to the balcony." She said, "I want you to pray that I will be healed." I said, "Well, you just go on up there, and they will pray for you." She said, "I have already been up there and I didn't get healed, and God told me if you would pray for me I would get healed."

I found out later that she had never heard of Toronto and never heard of Randy Clark, but when she got the flyer in the mail about the meetings I was going to hold, she heard the impression from God, "If you will go and have him pray for you, I will heal you." I did not know that at the time, so I was trying to tell her that I didn't want to pray for her. She said, "No, you have to pray for me."

Sometimes it is easier just to pray for people than to argue with them. Anyway, she was shaking, and she looked at me and said, "I have Parkinson's. I am in the last stages of Parkinson's. I am losing control of my bladder. I was in Kroger store the other day with my husband. I can't even walk without leaning on his arm because of what is going on, and I peed all over myself right in line. I was terribly embarrassed because now I am losing control of my very bodily functions, my bladder and my bowels. I don't have any short-term memory left. I have a two-year-old grandson that I have never held because I shake so bad that my child is afraid that I will drop my grandson. I need to be in a nursing home, and I can't afford it. I don't want to live if I have to continue living like this."

Well, I didn't have any faith, but I had a little compassion. So, I stuck my hand out, and I was going to say, "Come, Holy Spirit" and see what He would do. And I stuck my hand out, and I said, "Come!—and BAM—she hit the floor. Since she was on the floor, I thought, "Okay, now I can go pray for others." So I moved to where others were waiting and prayed, "More! More! More! More! Fire! Fire! Fire! Power! Power! Power!

But I kept looking over where she lay. She was still out. I was on the twenty-third day of the first 40-day fast I had ever done. (As a matter of fact, I have only done two 40-day fasts.) I was on day 23 of a fast that I started because I wanted to see creative miracles. We had seen wonderful healings, but we were seeing a lot of little children who needed more than a healing—they needed creative miracles. So, I was fasting and praying for a breakthrough for creative miracles.

So I went over to her husband whose name was Elvis—from Tennessee, by the way. I asked Elvis, "What's Parkinson's? What does it do?" He said, "It actually destroys part of the brain and the cells. He began to explain to me that the disease affects the neurological system, destroying it. And he said that you have 800 million brain cells, but his wife only had 50,000 left. I said, "Oh! She doesn't need a healing! She needs a creative miracle." He said, "That's right, she does."

Remember, I began by not even wanting to pray for her. I didn't have any faith, no expectation. But when he said that, I remembered that on the way to the meeting, my worship leader's wife had wept all of a sudden, uncontrollably. She said, "I don't know why I am crying." And I had not figured it out, but it was the gift of intercession. She was praying, and she said that she was so tired. She said, "You guys keep coming home and telling me about all these miracles that you have seen, and I haven't seen one. I want to see one."

So, remembering my worship leader's wife's prayer, I went over to Ann Harrison, who was still on the floor. I put my hand on her head, and I said, "I call those things that are not as though they were. God, I ask You for 500 million—no, that's the wrong number—I need 800 million new brain cells." And when I said that, she started squirming and grabbing her head and screaming and yelling, saying, "OH! OH! OH! It hurts! AAAA!!! OH! My head! OH! My head is killing me! Stop praying! Stop praying! Stop praying!"

Now, they did not teach me in my four years of college in religious studies and three years of seminary what to do next. What do you do when God is doing a creative miracle, and the person receiving it is screaming at you? I never had a class on that one, so I got a word of wisdom. I said, "OH! God! Don't listen to her prayer! Listen to mine! MORE! MORE! MORE!"

Now, she was lying on the floor, and I was down on my knees right beside her. The music was going on, and there were people praying everywhere, and it was loud. All of a sudden after I said that, she just went perfectly quiet. She was lying there, and she was not moving. I got down beside her and whispered in her ear, "Ann, what's happening?" And she said, "I don't feel anything. I don't hear anything. All I know is that you're here, Jesus is here, and Elvis is here."

And then she lifted up her right arm—a simple gesture, nothing exciting. But I was so happy because I knew what she was doing. For the first time in years she was looking at her hand not shake. Then she began to touch her index finger on her nose with her left arm. I was a little bit bewildered by this. Elvis could tell it, and he said, "Do you know what she's a-doing?" I said, "No, what is she a-doing?" And he said that is a test for Parkinson's. She has not been able to do that in a long time.

Then she got up on her elbows, and she said, "Elvis, get me a cup of water." So, he went and got a cup of water, and she turned around, sat up and drank that water. Elvis got happy and she got happy, and I was thinking, "Big deal! She took a drink of water." And Elvis said, "You don't get it! She had lost the ability to swallow. She couldn't drink through a cup, she could only sip through a straw."

Then she stood up, and she said, "Can I go up on the stage?" I figured God had healed her, so she was Queen for a Day. She could do whatever she wanted! So, she came up on the stage and got up right up in front of the people, right up to the edge of the stage. And at this point it's late, about midnight.

By the way, John Wimber taught me early on that often the greatest miracles and healings happen late in the evening. The reason is that the most desperate stay, determined to be prayed for. So I would say that 80% of the greatest miracles that we have seen actually happen in the last 30 minutes before we leave. Sometimes, it's the very last person we pray for.

So, it was midnight, and she wasn't shaking. She grabbed Elvis's hand and started shaking it. She said, "Look at this! I am shaking my husband's hand. Look at that! We have been spending $280 a month on my medication. Just think what Elvis and I are going to do with that money! I am going to go home, and I am going to hold my two-year-old grandson that I have never held."

Then she turned around, and she looked at me and she said, "Do you have a piano?" I said, "No, we have a keyboard." She said, "Can I play it?" As I said, she was Queen for a Day, so I said, "Sure! Go ahead." So, she walked over to the keyboard, and she sat down began to play, and she was good! I mean this woman could play the piano.

Well, it turned out that her husband Elvis was a singer, and he told me this story. "Randy, seven years ago I was singing to about 700 people, and Ann was my pianist. She was playing and accompanying me as I was singing, and all of a sudden she stopped, because she couldn't think of a chord. She couldn't think of a note—she just couldn't think. She couldn't remember how to make a chord. It just hit her all at once, and she was so humiliated that she ran out of the building. She had not touched the keyboard since that night until right now. We took her to the doctor and found out within the week that she had Parkinson's, and it already was pretty advanced."

At that point, Ann began to sing—and singing was her husband's gift, not hers. But she didn't care, and she began to sing. I will never forget it! "He touched me. Oh, He touched me, and oh, the joy that floods my soul. For something happened and now I know He touched me and made me whole." There wasn't a dry eye in the church.

I am so glad I didn't turn a principle into a law. Because if I had, I wouldn't have believed that she would be healed because I knew that I didn't have faith for her. What I felt at first was frustration. But God came and healed her anyway.

The Principle of Sin Blocking Healing

Let's move on to the second principle—the principle of sin blocking healing. In Mark 2, we read about the man who was paralyzed, whose friends brought him to Jesus, who tore off the roof of the house where Jesus was and let their friend down through the ceiling. Jesus, seeing the man, said, "Son, your sins are forgiven."

The Pharisees were upset because only God could forgive sin, and for Jesus to say that was in effect declaring himself to be God. They thought that was blasphemy, which it was—unless it was true. Jesus looked at them and said, "Which is easier: to say to the paralytic, 'Your sins are forgiven,' or to say, 'Get up, take your mat and walk'? But that you may know that the Son of Man has authority on earth to forgive sins...." He said to the paralytic, "I tell you, get up, take your mat and go home." And he did.

What was the first thing that Jesus said to this man? "Son, your sins are forgiven." Some diseases and sicknesses are related to sin. Some churches teach that if you are not a Christian, you can't be healed. Some missionaries in India, for example, have taught others not to lay hands on and pray for a Hindu or a Sikh or a Muslim unless he or she accepts Jesus first. Of course, I don't believe that, but there are people who do. Why? Because they believe that sin in your life can block the healing, which is true sometimes, particularly if you are backslidden and you are rebellious.

Woman with a Brain Tumor

Sin can block healing, but that is a principle, not a law. So, once when I was doing relief work, I visited a woman that the food bank told us to go and see. We were helping out, taking food to the poorest of the poor. She didn't know that I was a pastor. I just had a "Feed My People" badge as a volunteer. We asked the people to fill out forms that included a place for them to put church affiliation. But in fact, we already knew they weren't members of a church because we were only assigned to go to homes without any church affiliation. Our purpose was to go to the lost.

This woman's name was Terry Mesplay, and she was 25. She was not saved. She had been living with a man and had two children out of wedlock, now seven and five years old. The man that she had been living with ran off, after stealing her money, emptying her bank account and stealing her car. This left her totally destitute. On top of that she had terminal cancer, an inoperable brain tumor. She had tried chemo, but it hadn't worked, and the doctor said, "Make your will out; you are going to die."

Yet she had these two daughters, seven and five. She had been born into a Lutheran family, had been baptized as a baby and had gone to church once since then. The only prayer she knew was "Now I lay me down to sleep." She didn't even know the rest of it after that. This woman had no experience with the church.

So, I said, "Can I pray for you? I am a Christian and I believe that God still heals today." I didn't tell her I was a pastor. I just said, "I believe that God still heals today. Can I pray for you? I have seen people get healed when I prayed for them."

She said, "Yeah! You can pray for me." I started praying for her, and she said, "What are you doing?" I said, "Well, you told me that I could pray for you." She said, "Well, not now! Not here!" Many people think that when you offer to pray for them, you are going to do it when you get to church or when you get home. They are not expecting you to do it right there on the spot.

So, right now, until the culture changes, we have an advantage. We are going to surprise them. So, she said, "Wait until you go home." I said, "No, I won't do it." She said, "What?" I said, "You don't understand. God can heal you from a distance, but that's like graduate level healing. I am still in remedial school, and I just don't have enough faith for that. I am being honest with you. The likelihood of that happening through my prayers is not near as strong as if you will let me pray for you right here and right now. I have got faith for that."

So, she said, "OK. You can pray for me." So, I said, "Close your eyes." And she said, "No." There is nothing holy about closing your eyes; I just get nervous when someone is looking directly at me while I'm praying. So, I moved over to the side so that I would not be looking her in the eye, and I started praying for her. A couple of the women who were with our food distribution team there were also praying for her.

She said, "My head is getting hot." I said, "That's good!" She said, "You are weird." I just ignored that, and we just kept praying. Then she said, "I got electricity all over my head." I said, "That's really good." And she said, "You're really weird."

And we were praying and then she started talking. Yak! Yak! Yak! Yak! Yak! Yak! Yak! And she wouldn't stop, and I was thinking that she was not church broken yet. You know, she didn't even know how to assume the position. And I was thinking, "Gosh! She needs to shut up so that the Spirit can work on her. She needs to focus on what she is receiving so she can tell it, but she just keeps talking." And I felt like the Holy Spirit said, "Don't worry about it; this one is on Me. Nothing that she is going to do is going to stop this from happening." So, we just kept praying, and then we left.

Every two weeks we took more food to her and prayed for her, and every time for four times the same thing happened. Then another man moved in, and she called the food bank and said, "Don't come back anymore. I don't need anymore help."

I never knew what happened. Several years later when I was at the food bank, I saw her—still alive. She was a good distance from me, but I got so excited, I yelled over to her, "Terry! You're still alive!" And she ran over to where I was standing and said, "SHHHHH!!!" I said, "Well, you have got to tell me what happened." She said, "Well, do you know when you guys prayed for me and my head got all hot and electricity in it?" I said, "Yeah! Yeah! Yeah!" She said, "I went back to the doctor after that to get another MRI because the brain tumor had already metastasized to my breast and abdomen. They did another MRI, and they couldn't find one tumor anywhere in me except that there was kind of an empty spot in my head where the tumor had disappeared, and they said that the brain will fill that back in."

Then she said, "You know, I always wondered if it had anything to do with you guys praying for me." I told her more about healing prayer. Now, get this! This is the part that blows me away. I said, "Terry, it was the Lord who healed you. I am training a new ministry team at my church to do what we do. We pray for the sick. We are training a new team. Would you be willing to come and tell what He did for you?"

Now, who was I talking to? I was talking to an unsaved woman who was living with a guy, and she said, "Yes. I would be glad to come to your church and tell the people what He did for me." Now, something is wrong with the picture when an unbelieving woman living with a man is more willing to tell her testimony than people who are in the church and are Christians. People get saved, and they won't tell their testimonies.

We need to tell our testimonies because it is not about us. It is about Him. All of us are trophies of his grace. And so I want to encourage you to share what God has done for you, because it creates a culture, it releases faith. Somebody who might have the exact same thing or something similar can receive faith for healing as you tell how God healed you.

So Terry came and she started to give her testimony, and when she got to the part about making her will out with her five- and seven-year-old daughters because she was going to die, she broke down and started crying. Terry Mesplay at that time was not very far from the Kingdom, and I trust that by now the Lord has brought her all the way into the Kingdom. But if I had thought this principle was true—that sin can stop a healing—I would never have faith for people who are not saved to get healed.

But do you know what? I have the greatest faith and the greatest expectation for healing to take place when I go to the poor and to the lost. I see healing as a tool of evangelism.

Man Injured in Car Accident

One more about sin in our lives. A number of years ago in my last church, there was a guy named Charlie. In the middle of the service, while I was taking communion, Charlie's fiancé ran in and told me I needed to come outside to see Charlie. I didn't know who Charlie was; I hadn't met Charlie. Charlie had gotten saved a few weeks before while I was out of town.

I went outside into this little hallway, and there was Charlie. He was shaking because the power of God was all over him, and he was doing this little circle eight. He said, "I don't understand it! I don't understand it! I don't understand it! I don't understand it!" I don't understand it! I said, "Charlie, what don't you understand?"

He said, "Seven years ago I was in this car accident when I was 21 years old. I am 28 years old now, and I have steel titanium rods in my back. I have got screws in my back, and I have walked bent over like this for seven years. I have not been able to play with my little children. I have had pain all the time really bad, and my body chemistry is causing those screws to dematerialize. They say that I need another surgery, but nobody wants to give this other surgery to me, and I have been in pain.

Yesterday I went to the hospital, and they checked me and they stuck needles in my left leg in 13 different places, and I couldn't feel it. I came to church today dragging my left leg in to the meeting bent over like this. I was worshipping, and I saw this ball of fire coming toward me. It hit me and it went down my spine and instantly I was healed. I don't have any pain."

I said, "Charlie, come on! You have got to give your testimony." He said, "Oh! I am scared to talk in front of people. That is my biggest fear—to stand in front of people and talk." And I said, "I don't care what fear it is, you are going to give this testimony. This is too good." So I drug him into the church and up to the front, and he told his story.

My wife was so moved that she jumped out of her seat in high heels and a long flowing dress, and she began to dance before the Lord. That testimony broke us through into a level of worship we never had experienced before. That miracle released a level of joy and celebration in our service.

But here is the key I want you to remember. Charlie had only been saved two weeks. He was fully justified and barely sanctified. He didn't even know what was wrong from what was right. He trusted the Lord, and he got saved, but he didn't know a lot of what he was doing was sin yet. If people really get saved, as they learn, the sin takes care of itself.

After that Charlie had a problem, and he called me. When the power hit him and he received his healing, he had begun to shake. Now, he said the power was coming on him, and he never knew when it was going to hit. When it would come, he would start shaking again, and he would run and hide in the bathroom. He wanted to know "How long is it going to last? How many weeks is it going to keep coming?"

And I said, "Listen, Charlie, this is going to be hard for you to understand right now, but I am telling you, ENJOY!!! Because it won't stay forever, but as long as the power comes, don't be afraid of it! Embrace it! Enjoy it! If you need to go to the bathroom to hang out in the stall, that is all right, but you don't want it to end."

The Principle of the Anointed Person

The third principle is the principle of the anointed person. When I was really young, and still a Baptist pastor, I was pushing and wanting to have a breakthrough in healing. The only thing I knew was that I had been healed of severe car accident injuries, and I was pushing in.

I wanted a breakthrough in healing. So I went to the hospital in southern Illinois in a coal mining community, and I prayed for this guy. While I was praying for him, I heard a woman moaning across the hallway. So I went and knocked on her door, and she invited me in. I said, "Hi! My name is Randy Clark, and I'm a Baptist pastor. I heard you moaning and I know you are in pain, and I believe that God can heal and I want to pray for you. Can I pray for you?"

She said, "No! You can't." I said, "Well, why not?" She said, "Because I don't believe that it would do any good." I said, "Well, you may be right and probably are, but you don't have anything to lose." She told me she was a coal miner, and the roof had caved in and it had amputated her leg, and she had a spinal injury and severe pain. She was really in a lot of pain, and she said, "Listen! I believed that if I got to Tulsa to camp meeting and had Kenneth Hagin, Brother Hagin, pray for me, I would be healed. And I went, and he prayed for me and I wasn't healed. And if I wasn't healed when Brother Hagin prayed for me, I am not about to be healed when you pray for me."

Now, this is a principle—there ARE anointed people. Brother Hagin was one of the anointed men of God who had a really powerful ministry of healing. I honor him. This story is not meant in anyway to disparage his name because he really did have a powerful ministry of healing. He heard the Lord; he was very intimate with the Lord.

Anyway, I said, "You don't have anything to lose. Just let me pray for you." So, finally she said, "Okay. Go ahead." So I prayed for her, and her headaches and severe pain left. This shocked her and me because there was hardly any faith in the room, and I wasn't the anointed person. In fact, this was one of the first healings I ever saw in my life. And there are people who truly have the gift of healing, although everybody can be used for healing in Jesus' name. But if I had turned that principle into a law, I would say, "Well, I am not one of those guys. Who am I to pray for the sick?"

But I have never believed that God could only use God's men and women of power for the hour. I have always believed that we have been invited into the ministry of healing by praying for the sick. As one of my friends said, the essence of my message can be summed up in one sentence: "More people get healed when more people pray for healing."

Remember, God can use little ole me. You don't have to be the anointed person of God to pray for the sick.

Woman with Crohn's Disease

When I was in England at a meeting of about a thousand people, I was praying for the sick. A woman there heard me speak about someone in Anaheim, California, that I had prayed for who was healed of Crohn's Disease. Her unbelieving sister had the same thing. The believing sister felt heat coming into her abdominal area, fell off her seat and went to call her mother. She said, "We have to get my sister to come to church. I believe that God will heal her if she will come."

So, they called her sister, and the first miracle was that she came to church, which she never did. We had a team there, all praying for the sick, but somehow, when I came to the sister with Crohn's Disease, I accidentally skipped her. I didn't do it on purpose. I didn't even know I had done it. I would not know it until this day had they not written me a letter.

When that happened, as the believing sister wrote me, "I wanted to call out to you and say, 'Randy, come back here! You have got to pray for my sister!' But the Holy Spirit said to me, 'Don't look to the man, look to Me.' So, I didn't call for you to come back, and you went on. But I began to pray, God, if it is not Randy, bring the senior pastor, Wes Richards, and if it is not Wes, bring one of the associate pastors, and if it is not him, bring at least one of the elders."

But who stepped up? The youngest person on the ministry team that we had trained skipped up to her, a girl just 13 or 15, and said, "Can I pray for you?" And the believing sister thought in her heart, "Oh, no God! Not a teenaged girl—at least an elder!" But sometimes the un-churched, unsaved actually believe more than those who have been trained in churches in unbelief. What we have sometimes is believing unbelievers and unbelieving believers. An unbelieving believer won't see as much of the miraculous as a believing unbeliever, in my opinion.

So, the little girl put her hand on the woman's abdominal area, and she began to pray and the woman was healed of incurable Crohn's Disease. Within just a few weeks, the woman was back at work, and I got a letter from her sister eight months later. But the important point is this: there are anointed people, but God will often do the greatest miracle through someone who is stepping out for the first time to pray for the sick.

The Principle of Feeling the Anointing

Two last principles. First, the principle of feeling the anointing. This is illustrated by the woman who touched Jesus at the hem of his garment. Jesus turned around and said, "Who touched my clothes?" He realized that power had gone out from him. So he asked "Who touched Me?"

Mark 5:33 says that the woman came forward, fell at Jesus' feet and trembling with fear told him her story. I don't think she was trembling with fear because she was afraid. I think she was trembling with fear because she was caught.

Now, how come this woman couldn't hide herself in that great crowd, that press of people around Jesus? Maybe because she was shaking. That's why she was afraid, in my opinion, because she was the only one sitting there when He said, "Who touched Me?"

He looked around, and she was the only one sitting there shaking. Because He felt virtue come out of Him, and it went into her. You know, often that happens—feeling the anointing. There are times when you actually can feel the anointing. William Branham felt it in his hand. Oral Roberts felt it in his hand.

Anointing for a Missionary

Once I prayed for a man at a meeting who was preparing to be a missionary, but I didn't know that. There were a lot of people to pray for, and I was moving quickly down the line. He came up, and I said, "Put your hand out," and I just touched his hand and said, "I bless you," and I walked on.

I didn't know that he had driven several hours to get there, that he was hoping to receive more than just that simple prayer. I didn't know he was headed for a Muslim country as a missionary, but God did. If I had known those things, I would have spent more time with him.

So, anyway I moved on, and he was mad at me. But all of a sudden, he realized, "Well, wait a minute, that's burning." The burning sensation just kept growing until the whole palm of his hand was hot.

He went off to do his missionary work with an evangelical group, but the mission failed and they closed it down. But by faith he stayed. And every time the palm of his hand gets hot, he knows that God wants to heal somebody, and he will say, "Who is sick?" He knows God wants to heal when he receives that sign.

That doesn't happen to me. I don't think that is quite fair; it would be such an advantage. So some people feel the anointing. But what if you don't feel the anointing? Don't make a principle out of it. If you only have faith that somebody will get healed when you can feel the anointing, then you've turned this principle into a law. So pray anyway, whether or not you can feel the anointing—and let God move as He will.

The Principle of Moving with Compassion

Now, the last principle. In Matthew 14:14, and other places, the scripture says Jesus was moved by compassion, and He healed the sick. If faith is the greatest principle of all, this one is the next greatest—moving with compassion. Follow your heart.

Many of the healings that I have seen are directed to somebody just by a tug of the heart. I don't know why. But when you begin to talk to somebody and find out they have this problem, then you want to pray for them. This is just the way the Spirit has led me. So I believe it is true.

I was in Minneapolis/St. Paul for the first time, about six months after the renewal in Toronto. At that point, I had hardly ever traveled, but I was nearing the end of 30 days travel in a row. I was tired. I was exhausted, and this was the last meeting before I was going home. I was missing my wife and my four children who were one, three, eight and twelve at the time.

On top of it all, I was staying in the home of someone from the church—in the unfinished basement of a small house. It had a commode that didn't work right to begin with and sprayed water everywhere when I broke it. My associate and I had to get towels to sop up the water. It was a dark, dingy, yucky place.

It was not a good point in my life. I was discouraged. And besides that, the meeting was one of the weirdest meetings we had that year.

At the meeting, we had about 2,000 people in this big old Penney's building that we had rented. There were two people involved with the occult or something who were all dressed in black with black stuff all over them. One woman would run into the crowd with a big 32-ounce cup full of water and dump it over somebody's head then run away while the people in charge tried to catch her. Another guy would go up to any empty mic and start cussing. There was some warfare in this meeting.

Anyway, it was weird, and so I was preaching that night and I got to the end. After the invitation, I said, "Now, how many of you want to receive the Father's Blessing?" This always brought a lot of joy and at that particular time, a lot of people were getting "drunk" in the Spirit when they received it. So, I said, "Now, how many of you want that?" And I directed them to go to one area, and about 1,500 people got up and walked over there—three-quarters of the people.

For this meeting, we had about 100 people I'd trained to be on the ministry team, and about 75 of them headed over with the crowd. This wasn't fair because at that time, all you had to do was walk by somebody and say, "FILL," and that person would fall out and start laughing. Well, you could really cover a lot of people doing that FAST. And it was FUN. So did they need all 75 of them over there?

Anyway, then I said, "How many of you are sick and need to be healed?" The other 500 headed to the healing area with 25 of us to pray. I thought, "Oh God, I want to go over there, where it is fun." But over here were 500 sick people. That was not so fun. But then I sensed: But Jesus would rather have you here—where the sick people were.

So I went over to the sick people. I didn't want to, and my body language indicated that. The first person came up, and I crossed my arms and said, "So, what's wrong with you?"
I prayed and NOTHING. Another person came. I asked the same question. I prayed and NOTHING. Again the same question, the same prayer and the same NOTHING. Another one—same result.

Man with Hurting Toes

Then I got to this big guy about 6' 6," about 275 pounds and about 75 years old. So I said, "What's wrong with you?" He said, "My big toe hurts." My body must have said something to him because immediately he looked at me and he said, "No! No! My big toe really does hurt, and it is hard to minister when your toes are hurting."

I said, "All right, take your shoes and socks off." So he took his shoes and socks off, and I got a big toe in each hand. Now, I am a farm boy, and the only thing I could think of was the motions of milking a cow. So, here I was in Minneapolis/ St. Paul in front of 2,000 people talking to this guy's toes.

Because the way I teach and I pray is to speak to the condition. So I was talking to the toes. "Big toe, stop hurting! I command you in Jesus' name! Toes, stop hurting! I command the pain in those toes to leave! Toes, I tell you: Stop hurting."

Then I got this impression from the devil: "Are you aware of how stupid you look right now?" And I said, "Yes. I hope that nobody I went to high school with is here tonight."

At that point, I got overwhelmed with depression, despair, discouragement. I had prayed for five, and none of them had gotten healed, and there were 495 to go. I thought, "God, I don't want to do this anymore. I want to quit." But I didn't say that out loud.

I realized I was in trouble, so I knew what I needed to do was go into what is called "Secret Preacher Prayer." Unless you are a preacher, you have never heard of secret preacher prayer, but I'll tell you what it is. Secret preacher prayer is the kind of prayer the preacher prays that is so honest that it has to be prayed in secret. Why? Because if anyone else heard it, it would suck all the faith completely out of the room.

So, I went into my secret preacher prayer, and underneath my breath I was saying, "Lord, the Bible says that we are to co-labor together with You. I am here, WHERE ARE YOU? Nothing is happening, and I don't want to do this anymore, Lord. This is not working. I want to go back to the dungeon, I mean the basement, and put the covers over my head until I can go home tomorrow. I don't want to do this anymore, God. Where are You at?"

And the Lord took me into one of the few open visions that I have ever had in my whole life. He answered that kind of prayer. It was an honest prayer, not too religious, but true.

In the vision, I saw myself when I was seven years old, when I was kicked in the head by a horse, which nearly killed me. You could see the hoof print in my head and my skull. I was a half mile away from home and I had to run there with blood running down my face. My dad took me to the doctor who said if the hoof had been quarter of an inch closer or you had turned your head, you would be dead.

Can you imagine how fearful I was of horses after that? It wasn't until I was 12 that I started to ride again. And my dad said to me, "Son, if that horse throws you, you must get up and get back on it and ride it, or you will never ride again. Fear will take over." And then the vision ended.

I knew exactly how to interpret it. I knew exactly what it meant. God used the natural to explain the spiritual. He was saying, "If you stop now, if you go to the house now, you have been thrown with guilt and shame and all this stuff coming, and you may never pray for the sick again."

I knew this was from the Lord, and I tell you, I encouraged myself in the Lord. I knew He had heard my prayer. And so, I came out of secret preacher prayer and went back into normal prayer. "Big toes, in the name of Jesus, I command you to stop hurting!"

I went on, and we prayed for everybody, and a lot of the people did get healed. Then I went over to the other section where the people were waiting for the Father's Blessing, and there were only a few people left. I got to pray for one person who went "Ha Ha Ho Ho He He" and fell. And that was it; that one was gone.

Woman with Lung Cancer

So I sat down, and a woman came over and said, "Can I pray for you?" I said, "Sure! Go ahead and pray for me." She began to pray, and I felt electricity go all over my body. I felt the anointing of God. I felt the presence of God. I hadn't felt it the whole time I was praying for the sick. But when this woman prayed, I just felt God's presence. I was being refreshed, and it was wonderful.

Then I got up and she said, "Well, you pray for me now." So, I started to pray, expecting her to laugh, saying "Okay, Lord, more!" But she said, "No! No! No! No! I need healing." She was a young woman about 28 or maybe 30 years old, and I said, "What is wrong with you?" She said, "I am dying." I said, "DYING? What's wrong?" She said, "I have 28 tumors in my lungs. I have got tumors in my neck. I have tumors in my lymph nodes." I said, "Oh, okay!"

So I started praying, and in a matter of seconds she said, "My lungs are on fire." I am so glad that I didn't go home! I am so glad that I didn't go to the dungeon that night. And I just kept praying; I kept blessing.

Compassion Fatigue

Now, I didn't feel anything myself. That was not my night of compassion. I had compassion fatigue. Every mother reaches this point with her children. Somebody has got to put a little love in you before anybody else can take more love out of you because you have given away all you have. You haven't stopped loving your children—you just have compassion fatigue. Mothers get it and so can nurses and teachers.

But when you are suffering from compassion fatigue as I was that night, the enemy comes and he takes the Bible and he says, "Jesus moved with compassion to heal the sick," and then he says that you don't have any compassion, therefore, you don't meet the condition. Therefore, you don't have any faith that God is going to use you.

Don't turn the principles that are true into law so that the devil can beat you up with it. Just believe when you don't have compassion, He does. When you don't have faith, He does. When you don't feel anointed, He is.

Faith in Jesus

You don't have to meet every condition. When I pray for the sick, my faith isn't in me or my performance. My faith is in him and what He did at the Cross.

When I don't feel anything, when I am in a bad mood and the devil starts beating me up, I just get on my knees. I say, "Lord, I know I haven't measured up, but it is not about me, it is about You. And Lord, I am asking You to loose your healing anointing for the sake of the people. Do not let my shortcomings keep You from moving and touching the people." And I have so much faith in His love for the people I'm praying for that I know He will even use me when I don't feel like I deserve to be used because He loves them.

One of the main reasons for writing these two messages together is to reassure every reader that pressing in for more is the key to seeing more healing. The more sick people you pray for, the more people you will see healed. And when those occasions do occur that you don't see any immediate results, remember that you are an expression of the love of the Father, so every person should feel loved. And that love will encourage those people to keep coming back for more. Keeping a record of the testimonies of

God's faithfulness will also serve as an encouragement, so with each new day, you'll be ready to stick out your hand and do it again.

Other books by Randy Clark

Entertaining Angels

There Is More

Power, Holiness and Evangelism

Lighting Fires

Changed in a Moment

Other Booklets by Randy Clark

Evangelism Unleashed

Words of Knowledge

Biblical Basis of Healing

Baptism in the Holy Spirit

Open Heaven

Awed by His Grace/ Out of the Bunkhouse

Learning to Minister Under the Anointing

Training Manuals Available

Ministry Team Training Manual

Schools of Healing and Impartation Workbooks

www.globalawakeningstore.com

In "There Is More", Randy lays a solid biblical foundation for a theology of impartation as well as taking a historical look at impartation and visitation of the Lord in the Church. This is combined with many personal testimonies of people who have received an impartation throughout the world and what the lasting fruit has been in their lives. You are taken on journey throughout the world to see for yourself the lasting fruit that is taking place in the harvest field - particularly in Mozambique. This release of power is not only about phenomena of the Holy Spirit, it is about its ultimate effect on evangelism and missions. Your heart will be stirred for more as you read this book.

"This is the book that Randy Clark was born to write."
- Bill Johnson

GLOBAL SCHOOL OF SUPERNATURAL MINISTRY

Vision

To release followers of Christ into their specific destiny and calling, in order to live out the Great Commission.

Structure

Global School of Supernatural Ministry is a one or two year ministry school with an emphasis on impartation and equipping students for a life of walking in the supernatural. Classes start each September and end the following May. Courses are offered on-site at the Apostolic Resource Center in Mechanicsburg, PA. Upon completion of each program year a Certificate of Completion is awarded. Students seeking additional educational training may do so while attending GSSM through the Wagner Leadership Institute.

Community

The GSSM student body is diverse in age, culture, ministry experience, and educational accomplishments. From high school graduates to professionals to retirees - the students come together seeking more of God. Supernatural power, passion and honor are key values of GSSM and are reflected in our worship, outreach and personal relationships.

For more information - or to enroll in classes - contact us at
1-866-AWAKENING or apply online at
http://gssm.globalawakening.com

globalawakening

For a schedule of upcoming events and conferences, or to purchase other products from Global Awakening, please visit our website at:

http://www.globalawakening.com